LIVING AND DEALING WITH CRAZY PEOPLE

THE ULTIMATE GUIDE ON HOW TO LIVE YOUR LIFE CRAZY-PROOF (LEARN TO LIVE AND DEAL WITH THE NARCISSIST, PSYCHOPATH, SCHIZOPHRENIC AND MANY MORE)

Table of Contents

Introduction

I want to thank you and congratulate you for purchasing "Living and Dealing with Crazy People: The ultimate guide on how to make your life crazy-proof.

First, let me start by saying that if you had the misfortune of getting involved with a crazy person you have my most sincere condolences and I do hope that this book will give you the insights and strength to not only break free from them, but to heal from the devastation they left behind.

I personally have had the misfortune of falling madly in love with a crazy person, a narcissist to be precise. To say that I went through a nightmare would be an understatement! Anyone who has dealt with these types of inhumane beings knows it is nothing like you have ever experienced before. If you don't know how to break free from them, the devastating marks of the experience can leave you wounded for a lifetime. That's how poisonous they are.

What you - a normal person - need now more than anything else is knowledge of what you are going through, or have been through, and an understanding of exactly what you are dealing with, in order to make sense of it all. While in some instances there may not be a cure to heal the crazy person, I can assure you there is hope of peace and happiness for YOU.

I hope you will find this book a valuable tool in helping you understand the crazy person you are dealing with so that you can start your healing process and avoid any future involvement with them

are for clarifying purposes only and are the owned by the owners themselves, not affiliated with this document.

Chapter 1: The 10% of the People You Will Meet

Here's a fact: About 10% of the people that you will meet in this lifetime have personality problems. That seems to be a huge problem, since you definitely do not know when or where you are going to meet these people. Yes, crazy people are definitely a part of life.

The Crazy People That You Will Meet

While you may wish that every difficult person that you will meet would just admit to being crazy, that is far from being a reality. The truth is that one out of four people have a mental disorder or would have this problem later on in life. It also does not help that a lot of people who have behavioral problems are not aware that they are causing other people pain, or are in complete denial that there is something wrong with the way they act, talk, and behave. It is also very possible for a person to have multiple mental disorders at the same time.

Your goal is to identify the destructive behavior and prevent yourself from falling prey to any emotional manipulation that these people may cause you. This book will give you a description of each negative behavior that you may notice in a person and will guide you in protecting yourself and the people around you.

What Can You Do?

Since it is inevitable that you will encounter such people, you need to be aware that they may cause you emotional, and possibly physical, harm. However, some are experts at covert tactics of shooting you down. What you need to keep in mind is that your main priority is yourself. It may not be possible to quickly walk away or ignore them when you meet them; however, you have a lot of means to ensure that they would not affect you and bring you down.

You need to remember that their negative behavior can only affect you if you do not have a healthy sense of yourself. People tend to deliver the foulest blows and hit you if you doubt your own rights and you do not know where to draw the line. These people target your self-respect and your ability to hold on to your values, so you better watch out for that. Having the right amount of self-respect and being mindful about the attitude that is shown to or thrown at you would definitely allow you to create a plan on how to deal with different types of difficult people.

Do Crazy People Deserve Empathy?

When you deal with negative and destructive people, it is very likely that you become angry with them or simply not care at all. However, no matter how difficult they have caused your life to be, you have to understand that there is a reason for their negative behavior. Once you get to the point when you try to understand why these people behave the way they do, you become mindful that they are not just the villains in your life but possibly victims as well.

There are a lot of reasons as to why people act the way they do. For people who are struggling with negativity, anger, and utter self-centeredness, it is very possible that they have learned to behave this way because this is how they were trained to act. It also helps to understand that most negative behaviors and the beginnings of a troubled mind begin at home and at a very young age.

When you think about how a person begins to acquire a destructive behavior, you may realize that they are victims as well, just like how all bullies are. With better understanding on what motivates them to act the way they do, you become better prepared to protect yourself.

Aim Not To Be Crazy Yourself!

You need to keep in mind that negative behavior becomes destructive because it has the ability to influence how other people behave. Even when you think that you have the best excuse to act aggressively toward another person, or that what another person said to you makes you doubt yourself, you need to keep your emotions and your attitude toward a negative person in check. When they say that being crazy is contagious, it is because crazy people demand that you act like them so that they can justify the twisted rationality of how other people are.

Now that you have all of these notes in mind, it's time to delve into the different types of crazies that you will encounter.

Chapter 2: Narcissist Ned

Ned is the type of person who seems to be only interested in himself — he thinks that he is good-looking and all the women he meets are interested in marrying him. He thinks that he is the best person to talk to about anything, and he annoys people because he never seems to be nice without a reason.

You have been into an argument with Ned once, and it went miserably. He made a mistake on a very important report, and as his teammate, you went ahead and told him that he had to correct his error. To your surprise, he said right to your face that there was no error when he last touched that document. "You placed it there and now you're pinning that booboo on me!" he screamed. To make things worse, he started telling everyone that you are hell-bent on bringing him down because you envy his success.

Now that he needs you to do something for him, he acts as if that argument didn't happen — as if he did not go around telling everyone how horrible you were and bad-mouthing you. However, you are quite sure that he would stop being nice once you grant his request. What are you going to do?

Understanding Ned

A person like Ned is called a narcissist because he upholds a malignant sense of self-love. He does not see anything wrong with him at the surface, but it is very likely that he is suffering from a deep-seated sense of insecurity. Most of the time, people like Ned have not come to terms with the reality that perfect does not exist — as well his fear of failure.

What makes Ned a very difficult person to deal with is that you see that he is leaving a trail of pain. His sense of self is so overwhelming that he begins to lack any empathy or sensitivity to the needs of others. Because of his insecurity, he would want to project his mistakes to other people, become controlling, aggressive, or even scheming in order to get what he wants.

However, there are narcissists who are not as grandiose as Ned. While they may still be self-centered, their selfishness manifests in a less obvious way. If you have a friend who always pretends that he is sick in order to get attention and get his needs taken care of by other people, then you have encountered the other type of narcissist.

Gaining Control of the Situation

The best possible way to deal with a person like Ned is to keep your relationship with him, but from a distance. However, if you have to deal with him directly, here are the things that you can do.

1. Don't let your emotions get the best of you.

Narcissists are masters of emotional manipulation — they can be sweet talkers or extra aggressive in order for them to get the upper hand and order you around. Just remember that you do not have to attend to a narcissist's every need in order to keep the peace. You also do not need to succumb to every argument that an aggressive narcissist "invites" you into just to enable himself to project his flaws to you. Keep calm and be mindful of his actions.

2. Consider the context carefully.

Narcissists do not always act the way that you may predict they would — it is not an all-or-nothing condition. Like any behavior, there are situations that trigger a person's narcissism. Now, it is very important to identify where that behavior is coming from. Once you pinpoint where the insecure behavior is coming from, you would know how to avoid it next.

3. Recognize your own feelings and validate them.

There are a lot of times when a narcissist may project their own problems onto you or manipulate you into taking care of their own responsibilities. When you feel that this person's behavior is leading you to doubt yourself or that you are being sweet-talked into doing something that you should not be doing, remind yourself that those thoughts are valid. Draw the line there and do not be afraid to say no.

Chapter 3: Sociopath Susie

If you think that Ned is the worst colleague that you have, you haven't met his friend yet. Susie is probably one of the people that you would definitely not want to encounter. The problem is that Susie seems to be well-liked by everyone. What is there to hate? She's well-dressed, successful, intelligent, cultured, sophisticated, and seems to treat everyone well.

What most people do not know about Susie is that most of the things that she tells about her life is a lie — and she is not one bit sorry about having to invent the events in her life to make other people love and/or like her. She is also single most of the time — her exes would swear that she gets what she wants and it does not matter what the method is. She does not care about other people. She does not know how to love. However, she knows how to put up a show.

The Problem With Sociopaths

The real trouble with people like Susie is that they probably make it into the top executive positions of most companies. These people are those who are not afraid to undermine their colleagues in order to get into a powerful position, and they are willing to even take credit for the work that they did not do. They are willing to sabotage anybody who gets into their way because they believe that the results always justify the means. If it means being in the top 1% of the world, they are willing to bribe and steal from everyone.

Sociopaths like Susie are much worse than all the Neds that you will meet in this world because they are not only full of themselves; they also make sure that they have the best of everything, and they will not stop until they have created the picture of success that they have in mind. They are very meticulous about details, and they have the ability to create a "society" wherein they are on the top of the food chain.

Could It Get Worse?

Here is a very important thing that you need to keep in mind: Sociopaths are not psychopaths, but it is often said that sociopaths are simply unrefined psychopaths. Psychopaths and sociopaths are often confused to be the same, since both groups lack any sense of moral compass. However, psychopaths are those that you read in the news — irreligious terrorists, serial killers, school shooters are labeled as psychopaths because they transcend their need to exist in a society. When a sociopath makes the decision that he does not need other people to get power or that they can establish their own social order, then it becomes reasonable for them to lead a life of crime.

What You Can Do?

If you have the chance to walk away from people like Susie, now is the time. This person is definitely not worth being a part of your life or trusting with any investment. They are incredibly deceptive and manipulative, and they will stop at nothing until they get what they want.

However, if the situation can't be helped, what you can do is to be extra mindful of everything that a person like Susie does. It also does not help to think that you can change this person — this person is not interested in how you feel or what you think. This person is only interested in power.

It may also help to tell sociopaths that you are not interested in anything that they have to offer, if it means having to deviate from your own values and cause pain to other people. Since power is the only thing that motivates them, it may be helpful to make them aware that they are not getting it from you. When that happens, they will lose interest in you. Without them breathing down your neck, you will be able to get your peace of mind back.

Chapter 4: Debbie Downer and Anxious Ann

Debbie is probably the saddest person with the saddest backstory that you may encounter. It seems that she has had the worst tragedies possible in life — a bad childhood, divorce, being dumped by all her ex-lovers, the works. Her life seems to be a living hell, at least based on the stories that she has told you.

You can't help but sympathize with Debbie. How could you not side with a person that has been through a lot of sadness and misery? However, you sometimes feel that this person does not want to move on from all the drama and help herself. Sometimes, you feel that she is expecting you to simply listen to her sob stories and is not interested in finding solutions to her problems — be it from you, from other people, or on her own. You find it tiring to ask, "What are you going to do?" and just hear, "I don't know. I don't want to live anymore."

Ann, on the other hand, is severely nervous and you don't know how she will ever handle her presentation. She just can't seem to deal with the pressure of having to talk to another person, especially if she has not met that person before. She loses all her focus, even though you are aware that she can do the job very well.

How to Deal With These People

Depression is crippling to a lot of people — they are not just sad; they are way sadder than you can possibly imagine. It is one of the most debilitating mental conditions because it takes away a person's will to live and their ability to challenge their own negative thoughts. When someone you know and love is clinically depressed, you want to be there for that person. Still, keep in mind that your friend or loved one has a medical condition, so giving support may mean more than just offering a shoulder to cry on. Knowing that your friend has a medical condition will also ensure that you don't lose patience with him and don't get frustrated, if your advice does not "cure" his symptoms.

Anxiety, on the other hand, arises from unreasonable fears. The first thing you have to understand is that anxiety itself is self-sustaining. It causes problems with your mind and body that make it more likely to experience further anxiety. For example, anxiety changes brain chemistry in a way that causes negative thinking, reducing the ability to think positively, which in turn makes it harder to control anxiety.

Anxiety also develops physical symptoms that create their own anxiety - symptoms that can be so severe that they perfectly mimic what it's like to live with some of the world's most deadly diseases. Anxiety also creates hypersensitivity, which is a mental response that makes people more prone to noticing those physical symptoms and letting it affect them.

If anxiety were just nervousness and sweating, anxiety disorders may not be labeled as serious. But anxiety is a lot more than that, and the longer you live with anxiety the more symptoms you may experience.

The best way to help Debbie and Ann is to be there for them for support. Let them know that they can talk openly to you without fear of judgment. It is very important that they know that you're there to lend them an ear, and that you aren't going to judge them or change the way you think or feel about them based on anything they say - even if they recite the same depressed thought or fears over and over and over and over again. Be aware of Debbie's potential suicidal thoughts and ensure to stay close to her if she does have these dangerous thoughts. Volunteer to drive Debbie and Ann to their treatments, stay in close contact, even if it means you have to work extra hard to keep your them engaged. Involving Debbie and Ann in routinely activities that promote a sense of accomplishment and reward are great ways to improve the symptoms.

Dealing with Debbie and Ann can be very dangerous to you. While Narcissists and Sociopaths can actively hurt and abuse you verbally and physically, Debbie and Ann can affect you by pulling you into their darkness. What most people do is that they transform themselves into emotional crutches in order to help out their depressed and anxious loved ones, but this can be tiring and eventually detrimental to your inner core. It is important for you to be able to disconnect emotionally, not letting the depression and anxiety take hold of you too. Ensure to work on your own stress and problems, because the way you feel can have an immediate effect on Debbie and Ann.

It may also be necessary to encourage them to seek the help of a professional when they have disturbing confessions like wanting to end their life or that they are secretly hurting themselves (e.g. cutting). Help them realize that they could be wrong about the way they think about life and their value to the people around them — you know that they can achieve more things in life if they would only find a way on how they can tell themselves that they are special and that they are good enough.

While you definitely want to support people like Ann and Debbie, you have to understand that you can only do so much. Their lives can be improved only by helping them gain their self-esteem, which would allow them to have the power to challenge negative thoughts that keep bringing them down. With their ability to trust themselves, they would be able to get out of the comfort zones that their fears have built for them. Once they have gotten rid of the thought that they are victims of circumstances, they would be able to face their own problems.

Chapter 5: Bipolar Ben

You've been dating Ben for quite some time, and you can tell that you have had your share of ups and downs. By ups and downs, you are referring to his moods — he tends to be so happy and excited about the future, and then become depressed and self-loathing the next. You are becoming increasingly worried about him and your relationship — ever since he started having these mood swings, you have been feeling like you are walking on eggshells, afraid to trigger his foul mood. You feel inadequate and helpless, but you know that you have your great times together and you do not want your relationship to go to waste. However, you are beginning to doubt your ability to handle this relationship, and you are beginning to also doubt if your efforts are going to be enough. You are starting to feel inadequate. If only Ben remained happy, positive, and optimistic, everything would be fine.

The Swings Of A Bipolar

Ben is most likely to be suffering from a bipolar disorder. Most people tend to dismiss it as mere mood swings, but it could possibly be a lot worse. It is very confusing for a person to be extremely happy one moment and then extremely sad the next without a particular reason. Because bipolar disorder has a lot to do with hormonal imbalance and pent-up stress, people who are struggling with it may feel that they have to rationalize their moods swings whenever they occur. They often feel misunderstood and they often have to hide their feelings, which make their conditions worse.

However, people around them also feel as confused as they are. You may realize that you are losing your own patience and you feel that every happy smile and sudden tantrum thrown at you is a test on how long can you keep up with the intense mood swings that you have to deal with. You may feel that your emotions are being toyed with and it makes you feel that you are not doing your best, even if you are already doing everything that you can.

When you look at how bipolar disorder affects both the bipolar and the people they have a relationship with, you would see that everything that you feel is just a misreading of the situation. It is not about you or the other person — you are dealing with a chemical imbalance, which can be resolved by medication and healthy lifestyle.

What You Can Do

The good news is that Bipolar Disorder is highly treatable with counseling and/or medication. Living a healthy lifestyle also plays a big role in managing the frequency and intensity of manic episodes. The best course of action for a person like Ben is to first seek medical help. Seventy percent of people with Bipolar Disorder respond well to medical treatment. However, be cautious when you mentioning medical treatment to Ben — some people would deny that they need help or believe that they can live through the situation without being treated like a patient. If Ben does not want to see a psychiatrist to help him battle bipolar disorder, do not push it. Instead, encourage him to have routine checkups instead.

Also keep in mind not to take any of his emotions personally during his manic and depressive states. Remember that this is not about you — he is undergoing confusing emotions and surges of strength because of what is going on inside his body. What you can do is to make sure that you draw the line on how you are going to react during his mood swings and how you would normally behave when you know that he is himself. You would also want to reduce stress and triggers of stress and make sure that he is getting enough rest, especially during his manic periods.

While you would want to support a loved one who is battling with bipolar disorder by making him feel that you are with him in his journey to recovery, you may also need to seek personal support. Dealing with another person's struggle with bipolar disorder can be very difficult and emotionally draining and you need to have the means to release your own tension as well.

Also remember that you need to prioritize your own life — there is no way that you can enable yourself to support a person struggling with a bipolar disorder when you cannot provide for your own needs. It is going to be a tough ride through the mood swings and working to stabilize them, but you have to hang in there.

Chapter 6: Schizophrenic Sam

There is something definitely wrong about your neighbor Sam. She argues that she hears people telling her that you should not be parking on the road, and they won't let her sleep unless you move your car elsewhere. She also swears that you are being followed by spirits, because an angel told her that you are a descendant of the 6th King of the Ancient Aztecs, and because of that status, you should know how to act according to the traditions. By traditions, she means that you should not be driving a Toyota, but a Mazda — specifically an apple green Mazda, which according to Sam, is prescribed by your ancestor himself.

What Is Schizophrenia?

Schizophrenia is a disorder that displays the symptoms that you notice in Sam, which involves hearing and seeing things that are not real, thus making you feel that people like Sam must have a hard time getting along with other people. Contrary to popular belief, it is not a dissociative identity disorder like multiple personality disorder. While a person with multiple personality disorder may also hear voices, he hears these voices as a part of his self, as if he is talking to other aspects of himself or other existing personas.

What makes it rather difficult to deal with people who are suffering from schizophrenia is that it is hard to establish to them that they are experiencing things that are far from real. That is because their minds operate differently and of course, they are experiencing illusions and hallucinations that they think are very valid and real because they see and hear them.

How To Deal With Schizophrenics

When you are dealing with people who have an altered sense of perception, you have to keep in mind that you are still dealing with regular people, except that they have a different sense of perception. It is not their fault that what they see and hear is different from yours, and there is no use in telling them that your reality is more valid than theirs. Schizophrenics, as well as people with multiple personality disorders, can be very intelligent and creative people, and may even be capable of living very successful lives.

If you have to communicate with these people, keep in mind that it is possible for them to be easily surprised — remember that they are also seeing and hearing other things that you may not be aware of. It would be best to talk to them slowly in order to notice and hear you better.

While schizophrenics and people with multiple personality disorder are not considered to be dangerous, it may be a good idea to have one of his family member with you. A physician may ask family members to talk to a therapist, who will teach family members coping strategies. Family members may also learn how to make sure a loved one knows how to stay on the medication and continue with treatment. Schizophrenics and those with multiple personality disorder may be extremely paranoid and careful with their surroundings. Moreover, it would be wise to know what types of moods they would normally have, or if they have a history of hostility. If possible, you may want to ask what kinds of "personalities" they normally deal with — the behavior of these people are widely affected by the illusions that they have, and knowing these illusions would help you communicate with and understand these people better.

Conclusion

Thank you again for purchasing this book!

I hope this book was able to give you a basic understanding of people with personality and mental disorders and enable you to create strategies and techniques that will help you deal with them better.

If you have a friend or a family member who is suffering from one of the described mental disorders, I recommend that you obtain as much information as you can find on the particular behavioral disorder in order to be as helpful as you can be.

When meeting a crazy person in your everyday life, you will now be able to clearly identify the mental disorder, better understand the symptoms, and able to apply the suggestions and tips you have just read. I hope you will find the tips in this book valuable and I hope they will help you make your life crazy-proof.

Finally, if you enjoyed this book, I would greatly appreciate your book review on Amazon.com.

Thank you and good luck!

Preview Of 'GMO Free Diet: The Ultimate Guide on Avoiding GMO Foods and keeping Your Family Healthy with a GMO Free Diet' by Michael Skinner

Busting the GMO Myths

Myth #01: GMOs increase the yield potential of the crop

Truth #01: GMOs DO NOT increase yield potential, they may even decrease yield potential of the crop.

High yield is regarded as a complex genetic potential that is based on multi-faceted genetic function. Therefore, increased yield can never be genetically engineered in any crop. Data obtained by earthopensource.org show that the non-GMO agricultural productivity in Western Europe is much better than the GMO productivity in the US. Agroecological practices and conventional breeding are still considered two of the top reasons for productive agricultural yields.

The US Department of Agricultural has released a report that contradicts this particular myth. According to a USDA report of 2002, 'commercially available, genetically modified crops do not show increase yield potential.' Another report in 2014 stated GE (genetically engineered) has not shown any augmentation in yield potentials. Moreover, the herbicide-tolerant seeds may offer lower yields if they contain BT or HT genes."

Myth #02: GMOs are climate change-ready.

Truth #02: Climate change resistance does not solely depend on plant genetics

GMO producers have claimed again and again that crops, which are genetically modified can withstand any severe weather conditions. However, this is completely false as weather resistance of crops highly depends on the complex and invariable genetic traits. Moreover, conventional breeding of crops is still way far ahead than genetic engineering when it comes to delivering crops that are truly climate-ready. Tolerance to climate change partly lies in agroecological techniques widely used today. Some commonly used techniques to prepare crops in extreme weather situations include diversity crop planting and soil building.

Myth #03: GMOs can help farmers reduce the use of pesticides/herbicides

Truth #03: GMOs prompt the use of more pesticides/herbicides

GMO producers have claimed that the production of GMO crops decreases the use of pesticides. However, this is completely untrue. Herbicide-tolerant GMOs make use of a significant amount of glyphosate-based chemicals (e.g. Roundup), which technically is a herbicide. In other words, the reduced pesticide used is replaced by a massive use of herbicide. Consequently, the growing cultivation of herbicide-tolerant crops has led to the production of 'superweeds'. This so-called 'chemical treadmill' in farming has been proven unsustainable and questionable, particularly for farmers in the southern hemisphere.

Myth #04: GMOs improve the nutrition content of the crops compared to naturally bred produce

Truth #04: GMOs have manifested nutritional side-effects caused by genetic alteration

"Healthier and far more nutritional value in agricultural crops" is the promise of GMO producers. However, there are still no nutritionally enhanced, genetically modified products available in the market. Moreover, due to the miscalculated effects caused by genetic engineering, there are now studies proving that GMO products are far less nutritious than their naturally grown counterparts. 'Biofortified' crops, such as the GM Golden Rice, are still not readily available in the market due to the ongoing toxicological testing.

Myth #05: GMOs can help reduce the risks of food shortage

Truth #05: Food security can only be achieved through agroecological farming

The International Assessment of Agricultural Knowledge, Science and Technology for Development (IAASTD) report in 2008, which was highly supported by 58 countries, points out that GM crops are not the key to food security. Moreover, the report highlights that GMOs cannot be endorsed due to safety concerns, inconsistent yields, and restrictive seed patents. The report also expressed that food security can be achieved through the agroecological system of food production. This report was based on a four-year project sponsored by World Bank and carried out by 400 scientists from 80 different countries.

Please visit Amazon.com to read more about "GMO Free Diet: The Ultimate Guide on Avoiding GMO Foods and keeping Your Family Healthy with a GMO Free Diet"